CONTENTS

FUNCTIONS OF THE SKELETON

PROTECTION

Flat bones protect vital organs. Bones in the cranium protect the brain. Ribs protect the heart & lungs.

The cranium is made up of a series of flat bones

MOVEMENT

Movement occurs at a joint. A joint is 'a place where 2 or more bones meet.' Can be small (fine) or large (gross) movements.

The skeleton provides a place for muscle attachment. The muscles pull on the bones, attached via tendons.

KNEE JOINT

BLOOD CELL PRODUCTION

Long bones produce red & white blood cells as well as platelets. This occurs in the bone marrow.

STORAGE OF MINERALS

Bones store minerals. Calcium & phosphorous are vital for strong bones. + potassium & iron. Iron is needed to enable O_2 transportation.

released into blood

SUPPORT

The bones that form the skeleton allow the body to stand. It keeps us upright, providing a framework for muscle attachment. The bones are held together by ligaments

POSTURE

With the skeleton providing a framework, it gives the body the right shape.

PELVIS

FEMUR

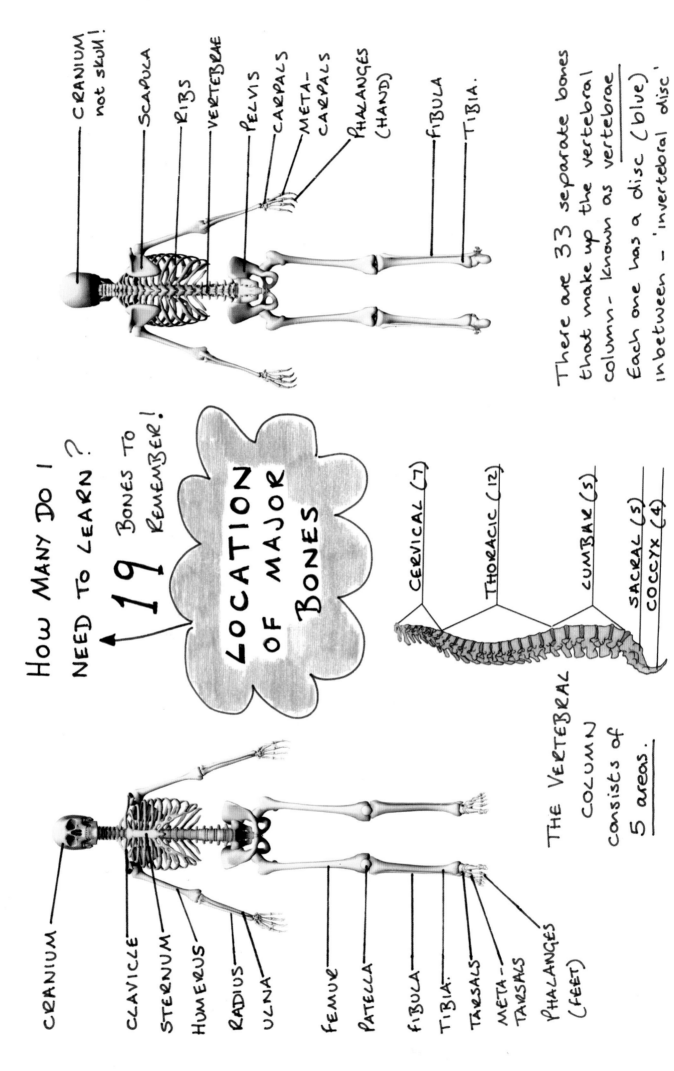

CRANIUM
not skull!

SCAPULA

RIBS

VERTEBRAE

PELVIS

CARPALS

META-CARPALS

PHALANGES (HAND)

FIBULA

TIBIA

There are 33 separate bones that make up the vertebral column - known as vertebrae

Each one has a disc (blue) inbetween - 'invertebral disc'

How MANY Do I
NEED To LEARN?

19 BONES To REMEMBER!

LOCATION OF MAJOR BONES

CERVICAL (7)

THORACIC (12)

LUMBAR (5)

SACRAL (5)

COCCYX (4)

THE VERTEBRAL COLUMN consists of 5 areas.

CRANIUM

CLAVICLE

STERNUM

HUMERUS

RADIUS

ULNA

FEMUR

PATELLA

FIBULA

TIBIA

TARSALS

META-TARSALS

PHALANGES (FEET)

2

DEFINITIONS

Synovial Joint - 'where 2 or more bones meet within a joint capsule & allow a wide range of movements to occur.'

Cartilage - 'a tough elastic, fibrous, connective tissue.'

Ligament - 'tough, flexible tissue connecting bones together.'

Tendons - 'a tough, flexible fibrous tissue that joins muscle to bone.'

ROLES IN JOINTS

Cartilage - acts as a shock absorber & reduces friction.
→ less wear & tear.

Ligament - connect bone to bone, keeping stabilising the joint, keeping the joint together. Absorbs some impact & prevents dislocation.

Tendon - connect muscle to bone & so allows movement to occur.

TYPES OF SYNOVIAL JOINTS & MOVEMENTS

CHARACTERISTICS

- freely moveable
- bones that 'meet' covered in cartilage
- connected by a joint capsule
- lubricated by synovial fluid.

How MANY? need to

know 2 - Ball & Socket
        - Hinge

Where they are found and types of movement that occur there.   Movement in 3 planes

BALL & SOCKET → 3 planes

the most freely moveable joint. found in 2 places. The HIP & SHOULDER → most movement.

The end (ball) of one bone fits into the dip (socket) of the other.

FLEXION, EXTENSION, ROTATION, CIRCUMDUCTION, ABDUCTION & ADDUCTION all take place

HIP - articulating (moving) bones are the pelvis & the femur.

SHOULDER - articulating bones are the humerus & scapula.

The bones move via muscle attachment. The muscles pull on the bones

HINGE

Movement in 1 plane

found in 3 places.

Need to know 2.

ELBOW & KNEE.

Allows movement like a door opening & closing.

ELBOW - articulating bones are the radius, ulna & humerus

KNEE - articulating bones are the femur & tibia.

MOVEMENT AT JOINTS

6 to learn & remember
- FLEXION
- EXTENSION
- ABDUCTION
- ADDUCTION
- ROTATION
- CIRCUMDUCTION

FLEXION

FLEXION - 'decreasing the angle at a joint.' Occurs at the elbow, knee, hip, shoulder.

In Sport - elbow - upward phase of bicep curl, preparation phase in javelin throw.

shoulder - at the end of a bowl in softball.

knee - preparing to kick a ball, running.

Hip - leg moving forward for a long jumper to land.

EXTENSION

EXTENSION - 'increasing the angle at a joint.' Opposite of flexion. Occurs at the elbow, knee, hip, shoulder.

In Sport - elbow - downward phase of bicep curl, release phase of javelin throw.

knee - follow through after kicking a ball, running.

Hip - leg kick in freestyle swimming. (upwards)

shoulder - arm movement of a swimmer backwards prior to diving at the start of a race.

ROTATION

ROTATION - 'turning of a body part about its long axis.' Occurs at ball & socket joints - the shoulder & hip

In Sport - shoulder - when swimming front crawl.

Hip - when driving a golf ball

ABDUCTION

ABDUCTION - 'movement away from the mid-line of the body.' Occurs at the hip & shoulder.

In Sport - shoulder - playing a backhand in tennis, raising the arm out sideways to perform 'the crucifix' in gymnastics.

Hip - a gymnast performing the straddle position.

ADDUCTION

ADDUCTION - 'movement towards the middle of the body. Occurs at the hip & shoulder.

In Sport - shoulder - playing a forehand in tennis.

Hip - the cross over leg action when throwing a javelin.

CIRCUMDUCTION

CIRCUMDUCTION - 'the circular movement at a joint.' In the shape of a cone, allows 360° of movement. Occurs at the hip & shoulder.

In Sport - shoulder - the action at the shoulder when swimming butterfly.

Hip - a step over in football.

ALL Synovial Joints have....
- a joint capsule
- a joint cavity
- synovial membrane
- articular cartilage

Bone

4

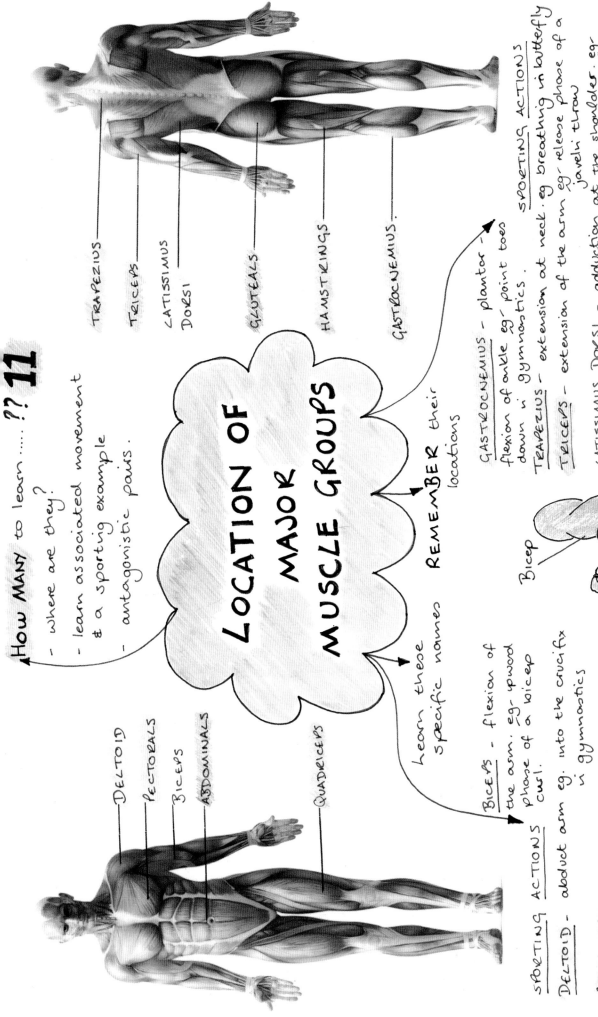

How MANY to learn......?? **11**

- where are they?
- learn associated movement & a sporting example
- antagonistic pairs.

LOCATION OF MAJOR MUSCLE GROUPS

REMEMBER their locations

learn these specific names

TRAPEZIUS

TRICEPS

LATISSIMUS DORSI

GLUTEALS

HAMSTRINGS

GASTROCNEMIUS.

DELTOID

PECTORALS

BICEPS

ABDOMINALS

QUADRICEPS

Bicep

SPORTING ACTIONS

DELTOID- abduct arm eg. into the crucifix in gymnastics

PECTORALS- adduction & flexion of the arm eg. forehand in tennis

ABDOMINALS - flexion of vertebrae eg. sit up.

QUADRICEP- extends the leg eg. follow through after a kick.

BICEPS - flexion of the arm. eg. upward phase of a bicep curl.

SPORTING ACTIONS

GASTROCNEMIUS - plantar - flexion of ankle eg. point toes down in gymnastics.

TRAPEZIUS - extension at neck. eg. breathing in butterfly

TRICEPS - extension of the arm eg. release phase of a javelin throw.

LATISSIMUS DORSI - adduction at the shoulders. eg. arms back to sides, straight jump.

GLUTEALS - extend leg at the hip. eg. upward movement of leg kick in freestyle swimming.

HAMSTRINGS - flexion of leg eg. preparing to kick a ball - football / rugby.

5

How does this work? within the muscle pair you have ......

The **AGONIST** or **PRIME MOVER**. This is 'the muscle that works to control movement.' This muscle **CONTRACTS**

and the **ANTAGONIST**. This is 'the muscle that works opposite the agonist.' This muscle **RELAXES**

so as one muscle contracts, the other relaxes allowing movement at a joint.

Muscles work in **PAIRS**. These are known as **ANTAGONISTIC PAIRS**. This allows movement in 2 directions. The muscles **PULL** on bones, they do not **PUSH!**

ANTAGONISTIC PAIRS

are 2 muscles that work together to bring about movement. As one muscle contracts, the opposing muscle relaxes, allowing the contracting muscle to pull on the bone (via attachment with a tendon).

FIXATOR MUSCLE - 'a muscle which acts as the stabiliser & helps the agonist work effectively.'

Each muscle must have an <u>origin</u> & <u>insertion</u> at the point of attachment.

<u>Origin</u> - end of the muscle attached to non-moving bone. eg - Bicep - Scapula

<u>Insertion</u> - muscle attachment on to the bone that moves. eg Bicep - Radius.

When the bicep <u>contracts</u>, the tricep <u>relaxes</u>, causing <u>flexion</u> to occur at the elbow. The opposite action causes <u>extension</u> to occur.

Examples you need to know......

<u>Hinge Joint</u> - <u>Biceps & Triceps</u> - movement occurs at the elbow. Flexion & Extension

<u>Hinge Joint</u> - <u>Quadriceps & Hamstrings</u> - movement occurs at the knee. Flexion & Extension.

6

NOTES

MOVEMENT ANALYSIS - PLANES, AXES & LEVERS

PLANE
PLANE - 'a flat surface that divides the body, into 2 sections / halves.

FRONTAL - top to bottom front & back. Abduction Adduction

TRANSVERSE - top and bottom

top = superior
bottom = inferior

rotation

SAGITTAL - top to bottom, side to side, left & right. Flexion, Extension.

Planes & Axes cross/intersect

MOVEMENTS ..... learn 3

where movement occurs.

Somersault - front or back, tuck or piked. Sagittal plane transverse axis.

Cartwheel - frontal plane frontal axis

Full twist jump - transverse plane, longitudinal axis.

※ information given on axes after seeking advice from ocr. This is their interpretation, not mine.

AXES
⊕ AXES - movement around an axis 'an imaginary line about which the body rotates/turns.'

TRANSVERSE - side to side, through the waist.
LONGITUDINAL - vertical top to bottom rotation
FRONTAL - front to back, through the waist flexion, extension top to bottom abduction, adduction

LEVERS
LEVERS - move around a fixed point.

Levers have 3 key components.

FULCRUM - the point around which the lever moves. is a joint.

LOAD - what you are trying to move

EFFORT - the force applied to move the load.

＋ LEVER - a bone

△ - FULCRUM
▢ - LOAD
⬇ - EFFORT
▬ - LEVER (ARM)

LEVERS
NEED to know
1st class
2nd class
3rd class

1st ▬ □⬇△
2nd ⬇▬□△
3rd ⬆▬△□

few in the body.
eg neck- heading a ball

eg in the ankle - calf raise

most common in the body. eg bicep curl. elbow

MECHANICAL ADVANTAGE
MECHANICAL ADVANTAGE allows you to move a large output with small effort.

Output > Input

component in the middle of the lever

Remember
1 - F
2 - L
3 - E

⬇ Effort □ Load △ fulcrum
3rd class lever

2nd class lever lengthens lever arm - bat, racquet or oar.

NOTES

THE CARDIO-VASCULAR SYSTEM

They all work together!

THE HEART

The HEART → a muscular pump that beats (contracts & relaxes) to move blood to the lungs & working muscles. Cardiac muscle.

BLOOD VESSELS

BLOOD VESSELS → move blood around the body. Arteries, veins & capillaries.

BLOOD

BLOOD → red & white blood cells, platelets & plasma. You need to know Red Blood Cells.

TRANSPORT OF O_2, CO_2 & NUTRIENTS.

function →

- moves O_2 to working muscles & organs.
- increased rate of O_2 supply during exercise.
- provides energy.
- removes CO_2 waste product. How? breathe out.
- nutrients from food moved around in the blood.

function of.....

Red Blood Cells
- carry O_2 & remove CO_2. HAEMOGLOBIN gives it bright red colour.

In Sport

High RBC count - high aerobic capacity V. good for endurance activities.

Low RBC count - anaemia, not enough iron, lack energy

THE HEART

THE HEART - is a 'double pump' system, or double circulatory system. Controls blood flow between - the heart - the lungs - others organs - working muscles.

This 'double pump' involves the

Pulmonary System & the Systemic System

comprises of......

Pulmonary System
- moves blood lungs → heart. Deoxygenated blood from the right ventricle → lungs via pulmonary artery. It is then resaturated with O_2. Returned to left atrium via pulmonary vein.

Systemic System
- blood containing O_2 from the left ventricle → aorta → rest of the body. The O_2 is used & deoxygenated blood returned to the heart (right atrium) via Vena Cava.

DEFINITIONS / TERMS

HEART RATE - number of times the heart beats per minute (contracts/relaxes) Ave 60-80 bpm

STROKE VOLUME - amount/volume of blood ejected by the heart (left ventricle) per beat (ml)

CARDIAC OUTPUT - Q - volume of blood ejected by the heart (left ventricle) in one minute.

Cardiac Output = Heart Rate × Stroke volume

Q = HR × SV

measured in litres/min.

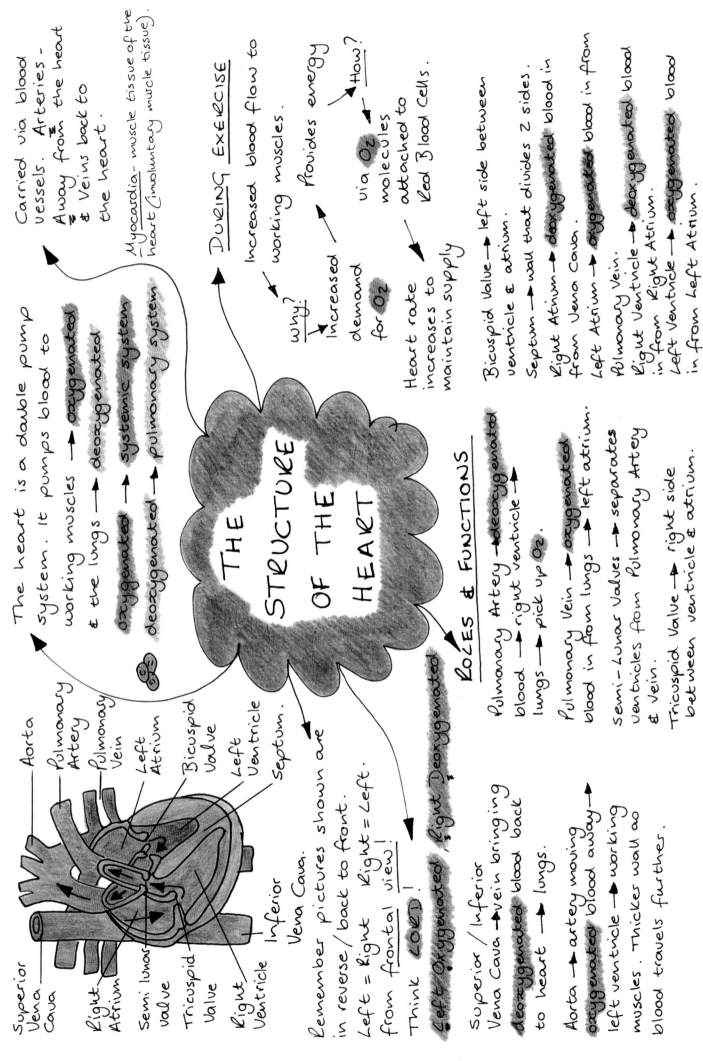

Carried via blood vessels. Arteries - Away from the heart & Veins back to the heart.

Myocardia- muscle tissue of the heart (involuntary muscle tissue).

DURING EXERCISE

Increased blood flow to working muscles.

Provides energy → how?

via O₂ molecules attached to Red Blood Cells.

why?: → Increased demand for O₂

Heart rate increases to maintain supply

The heart is a double pump system. It pumps blood to working muscles → oxygenated
& the lungs → deoxygenated
oxygenated → Systemic system
deoxygenated → Pulmonary system

oxygenated
deoxygenated

THE STRUCTURE OF THE HEART

Bicuspid Valve → left side between ventricle & atrium.

Septum → wall that divides 2 sides.

Right Atrium → deoxygenated blood in from Vena Cava.

Left Atrium → oxygenated blood in from Pulmonary Vein.

Right Ventricle → deoxygenated blood in from Right Atrium.

Left Ventricle → oxygenated blood in from Left Atrium.

ROLES & FUNCTIONS

Pulmonary Artery → deoxygenated blood in from right ventricle → lungs → pick up O₂.

Pulmonary Vein → oxygenated blood in from lungs → left atrium.

Semi-Lunar Valves → separates ventricles from Pulmonary Artery & Vein.

Tricuspid Valve → right side between ventricle & atrium.

— Aorta
— Pulmonary Artery
— Pulmonary Vein
— Left Atrium
— Bicuspid Valve
— Left Ventricle
Septum.

Superior Vena Cava.

Right Atrium

Semi lunar valve

Tricuspid Valve

Right Ventricle

Inferior Vena Cava.

Remember pictures shown are in reverse/back to front.
Left = Right Right = Left!
from frontal view!
Think COLD!

Left Oxygenated, Right Deoxygenated

Superior/Inferior Vena Cava → vein bringing blood back to heart → lungs.

deoxygenated

Aorta → artery moving blood away → oxygenated

left ventricle → working muscles. Thicker wall ao blood travels further.

BLOOD VESSELS & REDISTRIBUTION OF BLOOD

3 TYPES
- Arteries
- Veins
- Capillaries

ARTERIES

Thick muscular wall

Lumen; cavity inside containing blood (small)

Carry blood away from the heart under high pressure (oxygenated blood) except the Pulmonary Artery. In Sport HR increases, muscles need more O_2 → Blood flow energy. Blood flow has to increase. Walls of arteries contract/relax (helps regulate blood pressure), lumen widens.

VEINS

wider lumen

thinner wall

Carry blood towards the heart under low pressure. Valves to stop back flow. Blood usually deoxygenated, except the Pulmonary Vein. In Sport 're-cycle' blood bringing deoxygenated blood back to heart → lungs.

CAPILLARIES

very small

They are the link between arteries & veins - move blood between the 2. In Sport very important as allow gaseous exchange to occur.

O_2 ↑
CO_2 ↓

BLOOD PRESSURE

Arteries, veins & capillaries carry blood under pressure. Pressure from heart. Very important not too high or low! Test at doctors. Ave 120/80 mmHg. Top figure (120) Systolic - as heart contracts. Bottom figure (80) Diastolic - as heart relaxes.

REDISTRIBUTION OF BLOOD

Not blood shunting!

'When exercising muscles that are working need more blood.' Why? RBC's with attached O_2 molecule move there. Why? Source of energy.

Blood therefore needs redistributing away from inactive areas (digestive system) to active areas (working muscles) Blood pressure increases!

Important - do not eat prior to exercise. Leave 2+ HRS

Inactive - VASOCONSTRICTION occurs → blood vessels constrict (narrow) to decrease blood flow & supply.

Active - VASODILATION occurs → blood vessels dilate (widen) to increase blood flow & supply. More blood = more O_2

THE RESPIRATORY SYSTEM

KEY TERMS

LUNG CAPACITY - the amount of air (volume) the lungs can hold.

TIDAL VOLUME - the amount of air that is inspired & expired normally (breathed in/out) TV

BREATHING RATE - the number of breaths taken in a minute (normally Ave 12-20). Aka f Respiratory Rate.

MINUTE VENTILATION -

the volume of air that is inspired or expired in 1 minute. **VE**

therefore......

$$VE = TV \times f$$

(measured in l/min)

AT REST ..... breathing rate is slow & shallow (normal).

DURING EXERCISE ..... rate of breathing gets faster (increases) & depth of breathing also increases. Allows more air in.

GETS O_2 IN, CO_2 OUT

Inhaled Air	
Nitrogen	78%
Oxygen	21%
Carbon Dioxide	0.04%
+ water vapour	

Exhaled Air	
Nitrogen	78%
Oxygen	⇩ 16%
Carbon Dioxide	⇧ 4%
+ water vapour	

O_2 is moved around the body via blood, pumped round via the heart.

IN SPORT

Nitrogen - remains the same. Not used.

O_2 - decreases as used in sport or after exercise

CO_2 - increases as more produced as a by-product of respiration.

IN SPORT - the 'fitter'

you are, the more efficient O_2 intake & utilisation becomes.

WORKS WITH CV SYSTEM

Work together to increase O_2 supply & remove CO_2 efficiently O_2 in, CO_2 out = GASEOUS

EXCHANGE. The more efficient the CV & Respiratory systems, the - longer
- more intensely

you can train/exercise!

OXYGEN DEBT

after intense exercise - to break down lactic acid. O_2 needed to oxidise lactic acid ➝ CO_2. Deep, heavy breathing after exercise to repay debt. Only occurs with anaerobic exercise!

these terms ↗

THE PATHWAY OF AIR AND GASEOUS EXCHANGE

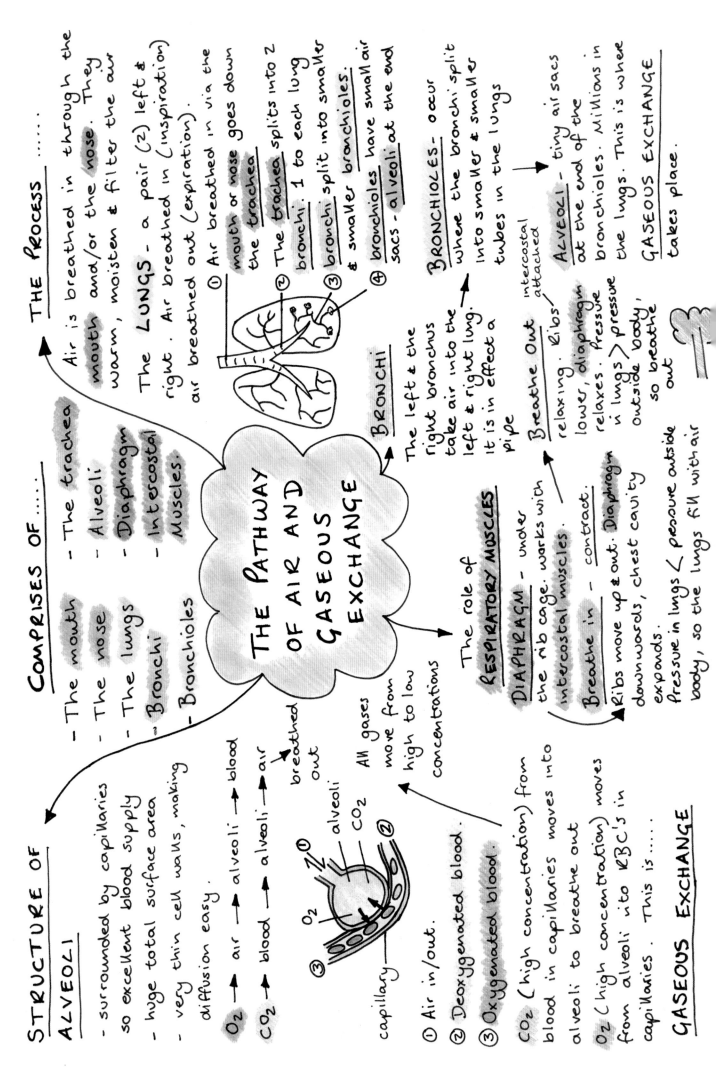

COMPRISES OF....

- The mouth
- The nose
- The lungs
- Bronchi
- Bronchioles
- The trachea
- Alveoli
- Diaphragm
- Intercostal Muscles

THE PROCESS .....

Air is breathed in through the mouth and/or the nose. They warm, moisten & filter the air.

The LUNGS - a pair (2) left & right. Air breathed in (inspiration) air breathed out (expiration).

① Air breathed in via the mouth or nose goes down the trachea

② The trachea splits into 2 bronchi, 1 to each lung

③ bronchi split into smaller & smaller bronchioles.

④ bronchioles have small air sacs - alveoli at the end

BRONCHIOLES - occur where the bronchi split into smaller & smaller tubes in the lungs

ALVEOLI - tiny air sacs at the end of the bronchioles. Millions in the lungs. This is where GASEOUS EXCHANGE takes place.

BRONCHI

The left & the right bronchus take air into the left & right lung. It is in effect a pipe

Breathe Out

relaxing. Ribs lower, diaphragm relaxes. Pressure in lungs > pressure outside body, so breathe out

The role of RESPIRATORY MUSCLES

DIAPHRAGM - under the rib cage. works with intercostal muscles.

Breathe in - contract. Diaphragm (intercostal attached). Ribs move up & out. Diaphragm downwards, chest cavity expands.

Pressure in lungs < pressure outside body, so the lungs fill with air

STRUCTURE OF ALVEOLI

- surrounded by capillaries so excellent blood supply
- huge total surface area
- very thin cell walls, making diffusion easy.

O_2 → air → alveoli → blood

CO_2 → blood → alveoli → air → breathed out

All gases move from high to low concentrations

① Air in/out.
② Deoxygenated blood.
③ Oxygenated blood.

CO_2 (high concentration) from blood in capillaries moves into alveoli to breathe out

O_2 (high concentration) moves from alveoli into RBC's in capillaries. This is......

GASEOUS EXCHANGE

SKELETAL
— with regular exercise, what happens? <u>TENDONS</u>... become stronger —

<u>AEROBIC</u> — with O_2
'Exercise in the presence of oxygen.'
$GLUCOSE + O_2 \rightarrow ENERGY + CO_2 + H_2O$

This is the most efficient energy system & with enough O_2 can work for extended periods (20 mins minimum)

Activities last for a long time — <u>20 mins +</u>

Activities are undertaken at a <u>low/moderate pace.</u>

<u>long distance</u> running, cycling, swimming
<u>60-80% MHR</u> (220-age)

<u>Energy Source</u> — Carbohydr-ates or fats. → slow to break down → needs O_2

<u>Waste Products</u> —
CO_2 — exhaled from body
H_2O — released through sweating

Exercise requires energy
Muscles need energy
Comes from food we eat
Glucose stored as glycogen
Back to glucose to be used during exercise

AEROBIC AND ANAEROBIC EXERCISE

Muscles best work <u>with</u> a large O_2 supply

Energy produced <u>with O_2</u> — <u>AEROBIC RESPIRATION</u>

Energy produced <u>without O_2</u> — <u>ANAEROBIC RESPIRATION</u>

CARDIO-VASCULAR
The heart, blood & blood...

<u>ANAEROBIC</u> — without O_2
'Exercise in the absence of oxygen.'
$GLUCOSE \rightarrow ENERGY + \underline{LACTIC\ ACID}$

Doesn't use O_2, therefore can only be maintained for short periods. During intense activity, muscles need large amounts of energy. The body cannot deliver enough O_2, so they begin to respire <u>anaerobically</u>

Glucose (carbohydrate) still the main source of energy

<u>Lactic Acid</u> — is a by product of carbohydrates being used without O_2. Toxic, causes cramp. Produced at high intensities

<u>Short, intense</u> periods of exercise — <u>30 secs.</u>

<u>Sprinting</u> best example (running, swimming, cycling)

finished — breathing very deep & heavy — repaying O_2 debt.
<u>80-90% MHR.</u> (220-age)

<u>WHAT</u> happens? — <u>ADAPTATIONS</u> occur — allows athletes to →

NOTES

Cardio - Vascular

What changes happen straight away?

Muscular

COMPONENTS OF FITNESS

WHY test fitness levels?

- Measures fitness PRE training
- MID & POST training schedule/programme
- Sets targets, enables improvements to be seen, aids motivation & can compare to normative data.

WHAT is included?

- CARDIO VASCULAR ENDURANCE / STAMINA
- MUSCULAR ENDURANCE
- (MUSCULAR) STRENGTH
- SPEED

Learn them All!

- POWER
- FLEXIBILITY
- AGILITY
- BALANCE
- CO-ORDINATION
- REACTION TIME

CVE

- works with the heart, lungs, blood & blood vessels to 'deliver' O_2 to working muscles.
- for a prolonged time without fatigue.'
- Strong heart → good O_2 delivery
- Aerobic system uses O_2 to break down carbohydrate → energy.

Vital for endurance athletes - run, swim, cycle. Developed by aerobic or continuous training. Test - Multi-stage (Bleep) fitness Test, Cooper 12 min run.

ME

- 'the ability to repeat a movement without becoming fatigued.' Weight training - low weights, high reps can develop more slow twitch muscle fibres. → delaying onset of fatigue.

Vital - endurance athletes, run, swim, cycling.

Test - Press Ups, Sit Ups.

SPEED

- 'the ability to move quickly across ground / move limbs rapidly.'

Can be
- leg → sprinter
- arm / hand → boxer
- thought → decision making by a rugby no.10

Partly genetic, though improved by training. (interval training).

Vital for sprinter, (any kind), fast bowler.

Test - 30m sprint test

STRENGTH

- 'the ability of a muscle to apply a force against a resistance.' Amount of force generated depends on size of muscle. Developed by weight training - high weights low reps. Vital for throwing events in athletics, rugby - tackling & weight lifting - clean & jerk.

Test - 1 rep max, handgrip test / dynometer.

COMPONENTS OF FITNESS

POWER

speed × strength.
'the ability to perform a strength movement quickly.' The ability to move an object or athlete up or forward.

Vital - throwing in athletics, high jump, sprint starts. Developed by Plyometrics & weight training.

Test - standing long jump, vertical/Sargeant jump.

FLEXIBILITY

'the range of movement at a joint.' Reduces risk of injury. Less likely to pull/strain a muscle. Increases reach/stretch, due to stronger ligaments & more blood flow → muscles.

Vital - hurdling, dance, gymnastics.
Test - Sit & Reach.

AGILITY

- 'the ability to change direction quickly & in control.' 3 main areas

- Core - lower to upper body
- Balance - full control
- Flexibility - efficient movement.

Vital - for a football/rugby winger. Test - Illinois Agility

CO-ORDINATION

- 'the ability to use 2 or more body parts at the same time.'

Can be - HEAD ⎫
         - HAND ⎬ EYE
         - FOOT ⎭

Head/Eye → heading a football
Hand/Eye → catching a netball
         → moving hand to hit a ball in tennis
Foot/Eye → taking a conversion in rugby.

Vital in racquet sports - badminton, tennis.
Test - wall throw test./alt hand wall toss

BALANCE

- 'the ability to keep your centre of mass over a base of support.'

Can be - static (still) eg holding a handstand
       - dynamic (moving) tumbling in gymnastics

Vital - in gymnastics, dance
Test - the standing stalk Test

REACTION TIME

- 'the time taken to respond to a given stimulus.' Vital in sprinting, be it running, swimming or cycling.
Test - Ruler Drop.

Learn all TEN & be able to link with Methods of Training (MoT)

20

PRINCIPLES OF TRAINING

Remember → **S**PECIFICITY
PROGRESSION
OVERLOAD
REVERSIBILITY

FREQUENCY
&
INTENSITY
TIME
TYPE

SPECIFICITY

training matches the activity, sport or position. eg long distance runner trains aerobically (continuous training). The training in rugby will differ for backs & forwards. In football a goalkeeper & midfielder need different components of fitness & so will train differently.

Progression & Overload

can be maintained by manipulating "how often" "how many sessions? Add 1 more.

FREQUENCY - how often - how many sessions? Add 1 more.

INTENSITY - 'how hard'. increase Heart Rate working at / add weights

TIME - 'how long' the sessions last. Train for longer / less rest.

TYPE - the 'method' of training. Add/alter method.

PROGRESSION is

used in conjunction with overload. Training must continue to become harder/ more difficult/more intense to otherwise adaptations to the body will stop. However, training has to increase in intensity gradually, otherwise it may lead to injury & reversibility

REVERSIBILITY

you will lose 'gains' to fitness if you stop training eg - may lose gains in CVE if stop running 5km 3 times per week. May reasons - illness and/or injury.

OVERLOAD

need to work the body harder than normal for adaptations to occur. However, the overload must be gradual. Too much, too soon may result in injury → Reversibility

Reversibility will occur. eg - a runner may run - more often
- longer
- faster / higher intensity

to develop their Cardio - Vascular Endurance. To overload the body you must manipulate the **F**
I
T
T principle.

METHODS OF TRAINING

NEED to know......
- CONTINUOUS
- FARTLEK
- INTERVAL
  - CIRCUIT
  - WEIGHT
  - PLYOMETRIC
  - HIIT

The following are all types of interval training.

CONTINUOUS
- non stop/no rest periods. Minimum – 20mins at a steady (low/moderate) pace. work at 60-80% MHE. MHE = 220-age. Develops Cardio-Vascular Endurance (CVE). Walk, run, cycle, swim. In Sport - Pre-season training for games players - high focus on continuous training.

FARTLEK
- a form of continuous training as 'non stop' though also similar to interval as periods of high & low intensity. Swedish for 'SPEED PLAY'. Involves changes in pace/speed & gradient GR8 for games players as works both aerobic & anaerobic systems. football, rugby, hockey - many changes in pace. Develops CVE eg sprint, recovery run.

Arms → shot putter
Legs → footballers
Body → wrestler

INTERVAL
periods of work, periods of rest. Rest can be active (walking) or just rest. Vital for sprint activities - run, swim, cycle & games players - eg basketball. work → rest → work Focus - time, intensity, no. of reps, no. of sets & rest period.

CIRCUIT
- can develop CVE, MS & ME. Complete exercise → rest → next exercise. 8-12 stations. Repeat 2-3 times (Progression & Overload) Work alternate muscle groups to avoid injury/fatigue.

WEIGHT
- can use Free weights and/or resistance machines.

MS- high weight/low reps
ME- low weight/high reps
1 rep - a complete movement
1 set - number of reps. (8-10)
Vital in speed, strength & power events. eg - rugby, throwing. Exercise muscle groups.

HIIT
- High Intensity Interval Training - periods of high intensity work followed by rest → repeat. 80-90% MHE. Overload - increase work time, decrease rest.

PLYOMETRICS
- develops power. Rapid & repeated stretch & contract of muscles. Max force, short time. Develops explosive -ness. Bounding, hopping, throw & jumping.

22

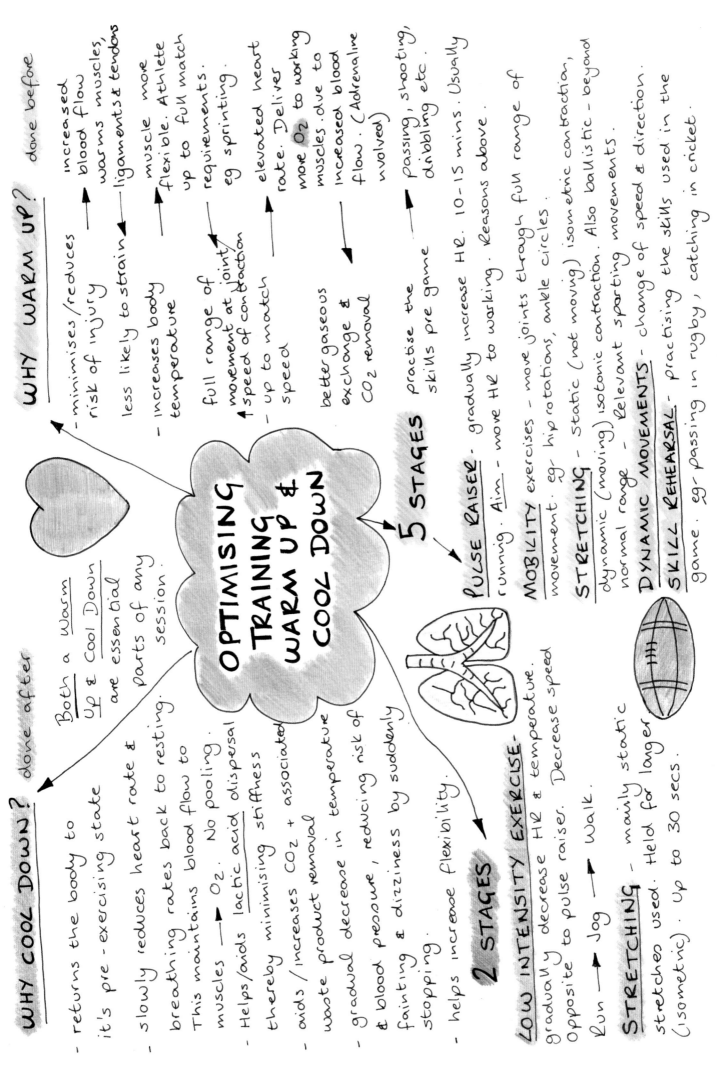

OPTIMISING TRAINING WARM UP & COOL DOWN

Both a Warm Up & Cool Down are essential parts of any session.

WHY WARM UP? done before

- minimises/reduces risk of injury → increased blood flow, warms muscles, less likely to strain → muscle more flexible. Athlete up to full match requirements. eg sprinting.

- increases body temperature

- full range of movement at joint ↑ speed of contraction — up to match speed → elevated heart rate. Delivers more O_2 to working muscles. due to increased blood flow. (Adrenaline involved)

- better gaseous exchange & CO_2 removal → passing, shooting, dribbling etc.

5 STAGES

PULSE RAISER - gradually increase HR. 10-15 mins. Usually running. Aim - move HR to working. Reasons above.

MOBILITY exercises - move joints through full range of movement. eg. hip rotations, ankle circles

STRETCHING - static (not moving) isometric contraction. Also ballistic - beyond dynamic (moving) isotonic contraction. normal range - relevant sporting movements.

DYNAMIC MOVEMENTS - change of speed & direction.

SKILL REHEARSAL - practising the skills used in the game. eg. passing in rugby, catching in cricket.

WHY COOL DOWN? done after

- returns the body to it's pre-exercising state

- slowly reduces heart rate & breathing rates back to resting. This maintains blood flow to muscles → O_2. No pooling.

- Helps/aids lactic acid dispersal thereby minimising stiffness

- aids/increases CO_2 + associated waste product removal

- gradual decrease in temperature

- blood pressure, reducing risk of fainting & dizziness by suddenly stopping.

- helps increase flexibility.

2 STAGES

LOW INTENSITY EXERCISE - gradually decrease HR & temperature. Decrease speed. Opposite to pulse raiser.

Run → Jog → Walk.

STRETCHING - mainly static stretches used. Held for longer (isometric). Up to 30 secs.

PREVENTION OF INJURY

CORRECT CLOTHING & FOOTWEAR
- clothing that is appropriate for the activity. eg. tight fitting clothing in cycling so doesn't get stuck in wheel/chain, studded boots in rugby/football

PERSONAL PROTECTIVE EQUIPMENT
- can/should be worn where appropriate. Can absorb impact eg- Bike helmet in BMX, mouthguard in rugby & hockey

RISKS & HAZARDS
- all activities carry a risk of injury. Risk Assessment prior should minimise the risk/chance of injury.

Purpose - check / be aware of 'potential' risks & take appropriate action to minimise impact.

HAZARD - is a potential danger or that may cause injury.

NEED to know the following settings & potential hazards: eg's

To minimise the risk....

SPORTS HALL
- walls (doors)
- doors
- lights
- floor

PLAYING FIELD
- litter/waste (dog)
- goal posts
- surface
- nearby roads

SWIMMING POOL (IN/OUT)
- chemicals
- equipment
- swimmers

FITNESS CENTRE
- broken equipment
- free weights (on floor?)
- mats
- other people.

ARTIFICIAL OUTDOOR AREA
- surface
- litter
- goal posts
- moveable equipment

APPROPRIATE LEVEL OF COMPETITION
- ensure that the activity undertaken is appropriate for the needs of the individual. Look at
  - Age
  - Skill level
  - Fitness
  - Weight
  - Previous experience

LIFT & CARRY EQUIPMENT SAFELY
- ensure use correct technique, bend knees, seek assistance, use machine if necessary.
- e.g - don't move trampoline alone

USE OF A WARM UP & COOL DOWN
- to ensure the body is fully prepared.
- Warm Up - start with pulse raiser + other 4 stages
- Cool Down - 2 stages - gets HR & breathing rate back to resting.

COMMON INJURIES
- include
- head injuries (concussion)
- fractures (any break)
- dislocation
- sprain
- strain
- Blister

May occur in any game eg Rugby.

NOTES

PARTICIPATION IN PHYSICAL ACTIVITY & SPORT

There are many factors that influence participation. Who/what affects these rates? Think of GASED!

In an attempt to boost participation Govt. Agencies & NGB's can promote the benefits of exercise & activity.

Ensure provision is adequate
in all areas of the country & that all have access to facilities. Can be affected by....

Discrimination
- on grounds of age, genders, race/ethnicity, socio-economic/class & disability.

Time/work commitments
- older = more responsibilities/work & less leisure time to exercise.

Media coverage
- male > female. Popular sports - football, rugby, horse racing dominate. Impacts participation minority sports.

Role Models
- children want to emulate heroes. Very important. eg- Adam Peaty, Dina Asher-Smith & Steff Slater.

Opportunity/access
- locality huge factor (choice) Near a pool or leisure centre? Transport to/from?

Environment/climate
- near 'the outdoors'? Access rock climbing, sailing - eg- Lake District.

+ Family - active parents, active kids - role models.

+ Education - being active at school.

GENDER
- most sports now played by both sexes eg- rugby & football. However netball still less media coverage. #ThisGirlCan campaign launched in 2015 by Sport England largely successful. Active Lives survey 2018/2019 gap men - women closing. 65% men } though still 61% women } men > women.
Why? traditional roles (homemates) eg. golf. Social side of sport very important.

AGE
- age restrictions on some sports eg- Boxing. Get older, more responsibilities, less 'leisure time'. OAP's - stereotype 'play bowls & golf. Social side of sport very important.

SOCIO-ECONOMIC
- focus on cost & disposable income. Equipment, clothing & memberships can be very expensive. eg- golf & tennis & so limit access by some sections of society. Working class & unemployed potentially limited due to costs involved.

ETHNICITY
- religion & culture can influence sport played. eg- cricket. Racist abuse still aimed at non-white players as seen in recent England football & cricket matches. Muslim & Jewish women not able to take part in mixed sex sessions.

DISABILITY
- much higher profile after London 2012 (elite). Barriers still at local/school level. Issues = access, equipment, funding, discrimination & sessions.

26

PHYSICAL ACTIVITY & SPORT IN THE UK.

SPORT ENGLAND

- focus - people & communities across the country to get a sporting habit for life!
- Protect existing sport facilities & playing fields
- Lottery funding
- Current focus/initiative/strategy ACTIVE NATION
- "... everyone in England feels able to take part in sport or activity regardless of age, background or ability."

YOUTH SPORT TRUST - focuses

- on power of PE & school sport to change young people's lives.
- focus - emotional health, obesity & youth unemployment.
  Primary PE & Sport premium, School Games Organisers (SGO's) & National School Sport week.

NATIONAL GOVERNING BODIES

- Independent & self appointed.
- Govern own sport. Aim - identify & lead body per sport. In - international, change grassroots → community talent identification, projects & safeguarding (hot topic!)

Dept for Digital, Culture, Media & Sport

- aim 'to enrich lives...'
- Vision - get the nation active & support elite athletes.
- support the UK's sporting interests abroad
- promote womens sport
- ... and more.

CAMPAIGNS

- This Girl Can
- Be Inspired
- Active Nation
- PE Catalysts
- My PB
- Young Health Ambassadors

Sport England }
YST. }

Useful websites for trends & data.

www.sportengland.org
www.youthsporttrust.org
www.uksport.gov.uk
www.thefa.com
www.englandnetball.co.uk

www.gov.uk/government/organisations/department-for-digital-culture-media-sport

CURRENT TRENDS

Active Lives Adult survey *latest version* May 18/19 report *latest version* published October 19.

24.8% < 30 mins activity per week ↑
12.0% fairly active but <150 mins activity per week ↓
63.2% > 150 mins activity per week ↑

Gender
men
65% active
24% inactive }
women
61% active
26% inactive }

Age - inactivity increases with age.
16-34 - 18% inactive
55-74 - 27%
75+ - 49% }

Socio-Economic
Professional occupations 72% active compared to unemployed - 54%

Disability - more common (41%) than for those without (20%)

Ethnicity - activity figs lowest for black adults - 56%

Activities - walking (leisure & travel) most popular → fitness, running, cycling

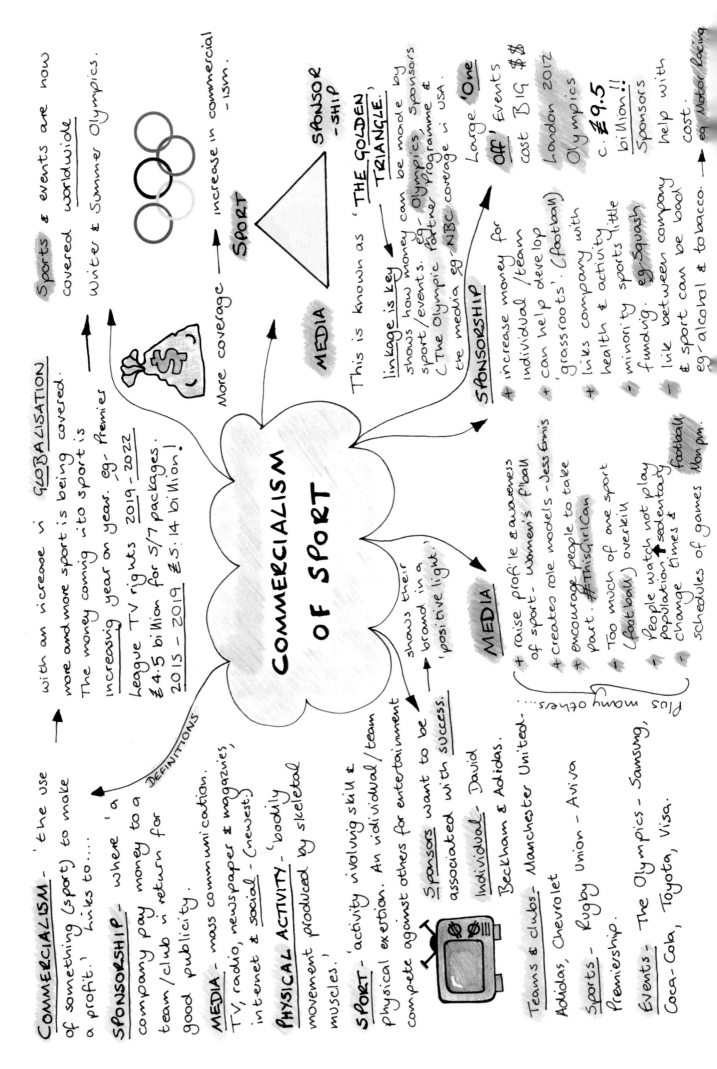

COMMERCIALISM OF SPORT

DEFINITIONS

COMMERCIALISM - 'the use of something (sport) to make a profit.' links to....

SPONSORSHIP - where a company pay money to a team/club in return for good publicity.

MEDIA - mass communication. TV, radio, newspaper & magazines, internet & social - (newest.)

PHYSICAL ACTIVITY - 'bodily movement produced by skeletal muscles.'

SPORT - 'activity involving skill & physical exertion. An individual/team compete against others for entertainment'

GLOBALISATION

Sports & events are now covered worldwide - Winter & Summer Olympics.

with an increase in GLOBALISATION more and more sport is being covered. The money coming into sport is increasing year on year. eg - Premier League TV rights 2019-2022 £4.5 billion for 5/7 packages. 2015-2019 £5.14 billion!

increase in commercial - ism.

More coverage → SPORT

SPONSORSHIP — THE GOLDEN TRIANGLE

SPORT / MEDIA / SPONSORSHIP

This is known as 'THE GOLDEN TRIANGLE.'

linkage is key shows how money can be made by sport/events. eg - Olympics. Sponsors & (The Olympic partner programme & the media eg - NBC coverage in USA.

SPONSORSHIP
+ increase money for individual/team
+ can help develop 'grassroots'. (football)
+ links company with health & activity
- minority sports little funding. eg-Squash
- link between company & sport can be bad eg - alcohol & tobacco.

Large 'One off' events cost BIG $$
London 2012 Olympics c. £9.5 billion!!
Sponsors help with cost. eg - Motor Racing

MEDIA
+ raise profile & awareness of sport - Women's f'ball
+ created role models - Jess Ennis
+ encourage people to take part. #ThisGirlCan
- Too much of one sport (football) overkill
- People watch not play ↑ sedentary population change times & schedules of games
Plus many others...

Sponsors want to be associated with success. shows their brand in a 'positive light.'

Individual - David Beckham & Adidas.

Teams & clubs- Manchester United- Adidas, Chevrolet

Sports - Rugby Union - Aviva Premiership.

Events - The Olympics - Samsung, Coca-Cola, Toyota, Visa.

ETHICS & VIOLENCE IN SPORT

VIOLENCE
- 'a deliberate act/behaviour with the intent to harm.'
- Steps over the line from being aggressive to being violent.
- eg. Mike Tyson biting a chunk off Evander Holyfield's ear, not once, but twice! Boxing, 1997. Zidane headbutt WC final 2006.

Why?
- aggression within game eg. Ice Hockey, 'enforcer' comes on = fight!
- equipment used wrongly as weapon. eg. hockey stick.
- unable to control aggression/arousal levels. Spills over into violence. eg. Rugby league.
- contact sport & someone 'oversteps' the mark. eg. Aussie rules.
- responding to crowd behaviour/taunts eg. racism
- provocation by opponent
- importance of game eg. football 'derby' match.

DEVIANCE
- simply put, is cheating. It is 'deliberately breaking the rules of sport in an illegal manner. They want to win & will go to any lengths to do so. eg. Ben Johnson using steroids to try & win Gold at the 1988 Seoul Olympics in 100m.

Other eg's
- professional foul in football
- deliberate knock-on in rugby
- bribing officials eg. FIFA bids
- match fixing eg. cricket.
- footballers gambling on games
- hooliganism Euro 2016
- mechanical aid - eg. cycling 'engine'.

SPORTSMANSHIP
- 'Play & abide by the rules. Win & lose graciously.' Sportsmen/women are role models. Want to win, but not 'at all cost.'
- Fair play, respect & polite behaviour.
- eg. kicking a ball out of play in football for an injured opponent. Paulo di Canio - West Ham v Everton, Paul Gerrard, Everton goalie lying injured, di Canio caught ball to let physio on pitch. Awarded FIFA Fair Play Award.

GAMESMANSHIP
'the' use of dubious, though not illegal methods to win or gain an advantage. Bending the rules to help you win. eg. the Australian cricket team 'sledging' English batsmen to affect their focus - gain advantage.

Reasons for DEVIANT behaviour.
- think others are cheating & getting away with it. eg. cycling, athletics
- pressure to win - from coach - why not?
- lack of moral compass
- gain an edge, an advantage - drugs
- 'win at all cost' attitude
- pressure to win - sponsors
- stress of competition - stress relief.
- lack of positive role models
- Deviant behaviour has consequences
- bans, lose sponsors (equals money) lose respect, illness & death (drugs!)

DRUGS IN SPORT

LEARN **3** /₃ (there are more!)

WHY use them?
- pressure from coach?
- enhances performance
- impact?
- train harder more intensely
- decrease recovery time
- physiological & psychological benefits
- £ $ €
- better chance of winning!

Taking/using PERFORMANCE ENHANCING DRUGS is cheating. It is a form of **DEVIANCE** - 'deliberately breaking the rules of sport (written/unwritten) in an illegal manner.'

ANABOLIC STEROIDS - mimics testosterone. Most widely available & commonly used.
Increased muscle mass & strength, power & bone growth.
Side Effects ..... loads
Infertility, high BP, heart attack, stroke → death!
eg- Ben Johnson Canadian sprinter at Seoul Olympics in 1988 took stanozolol.
used by sprinters boxers

STIMULANTS - 2nd most common drug used. Amphetamines. Stimulates, increases alertness, increases HR. Side Effects - Insomnia, increased HR & aggression
eg- 2013 Asafa Powell - positive for Oxilofrine - used by sprinters & cyclists

BETA BLOCKERS - increase steadiness, reduce tremors & HR - danger
SIDE EFFECTS - tiredness, depression. Used in Archery, golf
eg- Kim Jong Su - won silver in 50m pistol 2008 Beijing for North Korea. Had taken Propranolol.

Drug use impact on Sport
- creates a suspicious climate round all athletes
- Testing is expensive
- gives the sport a bad name - cycling & Tour de France
- Bad name for country eg Russia banned by IOC.

TESTING
- Blood
- Urine
→ positive → B Sample → positive → **BANNED.**

Best eg of drugs cheat- Lance Armstrong cycling.

Reasons
- Poor role model
- Lose medals, sponsorship deals.
- lose respect, career in ruins.
- Breaking the law

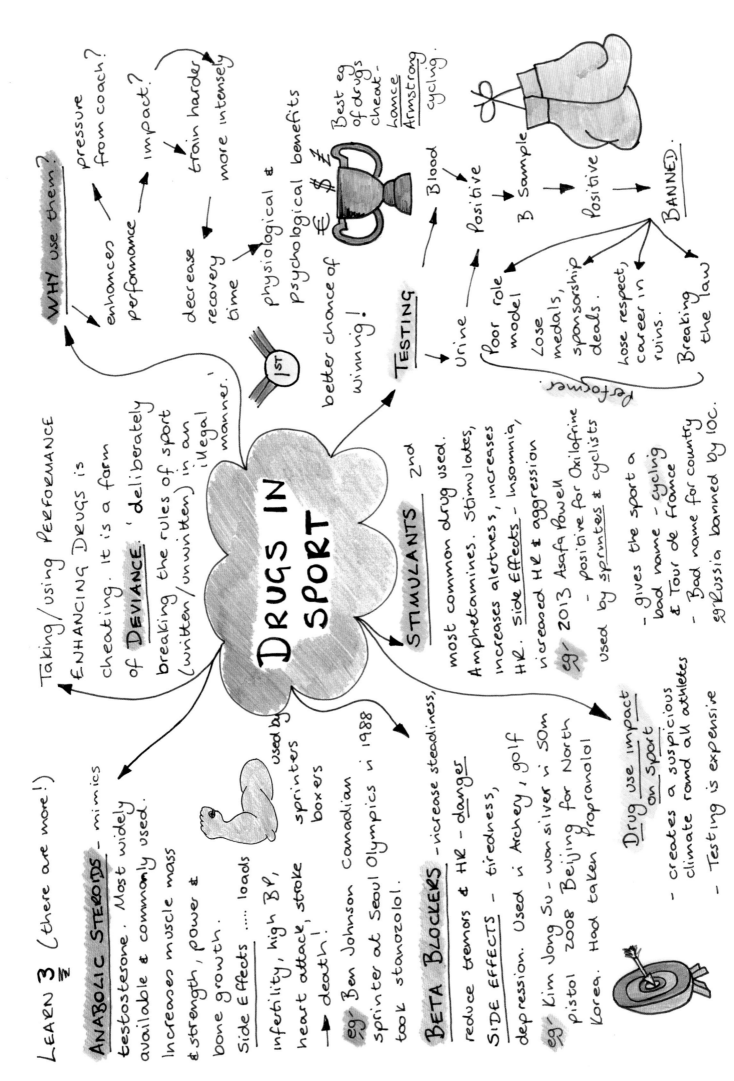

NOTES

SKILFUL MOVEMENT & CLASSIFICATION OF SKILL

MOTOR SKILLS
'an action that has a goal that requires voluntary body / limb movement.' OR 'the ability to perform complex muscle & nerve acts that produce movement.'

Can be fine or gross.

There are 2 continua to learn
- DIFFICULTY - SIMPLE → COMPLEX skills. The more thought/judgements made, the more complex the skill
- ENVIRONMENTAL - OPEN → CLOSED skills. The more the skill is affected by the environment, the more open the skill becomes.

Perceptual skills - anticipate
Cognitive skills - work out

SIMPLE
- a skill that is easy to execute. May be autonomous. Needs little thought or planning. eg - short pass in football

COMPLEX
- needs full focus, a difficult skill to perform. May be learnt in phases.

Much practice needed.

eg - a drop goal from distance.

OPEN
- found in 'team games, football, netball, rugby. The playing environment constantly changes - due to opposition, weather, teammates. 'team mates' practices would be game related eg - a lofted pass in football

CLOSED
- has a definite start & end point. Player controls the pace. Environment has minimal (if any) impact. eg - a serve in tennis, a lineout / a throw in rugby.

Short pass — Drop goal
SIMPLE → COMPLEX

Tennis serve — Lofted pass
CLOSED → OPEN

① Difficulty
② Environmental

SKILFUL MOVEMENT.
needs to be learnt! 'a pre-determined movement that is fluent & co-ordinated, efficient, technically accurate & aesthetically pleasing.'

Requires much practice!

Pre-determined - performer knows what they are doing. eg - a gymnast & their floor routine.

Efficient - no wasted time. eg - Adam Peaty swimming 100m breaststroke. minimal splash.

Co-Ordinated - All sections/parts link in & fit together. eg - High jumpers approach, take off, flight.

Fluent - the routine 'flows' and is smooth. eg - A rhythmic gymnasts moves flow into each other.

Aesthetic - looks good. eg - A great tennis smash.

GOAL SETTING & MENTAL PREPARATION

WHY? allows you to prepare for a game/match. Prior to warm up. Get 'In the zone.'

Allows sportsmen/women to <u>cope</u> with nerves & anxiety.

eg before a cup final, relaxation (quiet meditation) control HR, Positive self talk/thinking - encourage to perform.

Cognitive - affects mind

Somatic - affects body

Learn these **4** techniques

A target to focus on → improving in your training.

Gives you a target, something to aim for.

It is very good for....

IMPROVING & OPTIMISING PERFORMANCE

SMART goals may result in better training → better performance. Set numerous short term goals. When achieved, set another. Keeps you motivated!

EXERCISE & TRAINING ADHERENCE - with a goal/target, more likely to maintain training

MOTIVATING PERFORMERS

have a goal to aim for - <u>Too easy</u> - poor results from poor training <u>Too difficult</u> - demotivated

---

SPECIFIC - have a clear, detailed goal or target. eg improve 1 rep max by 10 kg in 6 weeks. Run 100m in 0.3 secs faster.

MEASUREABLE - can it be measured or tested? timed?

ACHIEVABLE - is it possible? 0.3 secs faster ✓ 2.0 secs ✗ in 6 weeks ✓ in 6 weeks ✗ aids motivation.

RECORDED - allows progress to be measured → Adapt if needed

TIMED - set an end point. 1-6 weeks gives an end target to aim for.

MENTAL REHEARSAL

2 main forms

<u>INTERNAL</u> - 'visualise' yourself 'doing' the activity eg saving a penalty, where to bowl at a batsman.

<u>EXTERNAL</u> - you 'visualise' the activity from outside your body eg riding Alpe D'huez's twists & turns.

Can calm nerves & improve focus ✓

linked

SELECTIVE ATTENTION

focus on only the important aspects, not distractions eg crowd noise when taking a conversion in rugby.

POSITIVE THINKING

'Positive self talk.' "I can do it!" Don't talk yourself out of it. eg "I can sink this putt to win the Open. I've done this over & over."

IMAGERY - used to 'calm nerves.' Take your mind elsewhere, somewhere relaxing

GUIDANCE AND FEEDBACK

INTRINSIC - self feedback from the athlete. How they feel they played in a game, or executed a vault.
Limited experience = Limited feedback.
Elite - can be very self critical.

FEEDBACK - is given with the aim of improving the skill or performance. Can be during or after the session or match.

EXTRINSIC - external or outside feedback given during or after the session / game. eg A football manager during a game, a coach after a session. Visual / verbal.

KNOWLEDGE OF RESULTS - at the end. Evaluates performance in a game (own & score), outcome in a race. eg 2nd in 100m Freestyle. Minimal learning - recap.

NEGATIVE - when a performance or result does not go to plan. Tell what was wrong & importantly how to improve. Can motivate. Useful - elite level. eg finish 5th 100m final

KNOWLEDGE OF PERFORMANCE - how well the performer has played (eg in a game of rugby) or executed a move, routine. (eg floor routine in gymnastics)
focus - quality & pattern of movement.

Positive External Feedback ???

Positive - 'praise! "Well done." Given for a positive result for team / individual. Or for particular skill eg pass. Good for beginners — encouragement.

GUIDANCE - given when learning or practising a skill.

VISUAL - show the skill you want performer to learn / execute. See / watch it. Can be demonstration, video, picture or graphic. Focus on main aspects, repeat.
+ novices
+ good to see
+ quick
- learn from 'incorrect demo'
- questions.

together.

VERBAL - tell the performer what you want them to do. Give instructions. Concise & clear.
+ good detail + quick.
- cannot see - hard to visualise
- talk too long.

MANUAL - coach & performer together. Physical support given. eg - tumbling in gymnastics.

MECHANICAL - use of a 'device' to support the performer. eg - a harness in trampolining.

Manual
+ reassurance
+ reduces risk
- safeguarding
- 'un-natural feel.'

Mechanical
+ reassurance
+ reduces risk
- dependant on support
- cost.

together

34

NOTES

HEALTH, FITNESS & WELLBEING

Definitions

HEALTH - 'a state of complete emotional, physical & social wellbeing, not merely the absence of disease or infirmity.'

FITNESS - 'the ability to meet the demands of the environment.'

WELLBEING - 'a feeling of being contented, happy, (prosperous) and healthy.'

SEDENTARY - 'being inactive.'

3 areas

- PHYSICAL - the body
- EMOTIONAL - (not mental!) mind & feelings
- SOCIAL - interacting with others.

All linked: exercise regularly, keep a healthy balanced diet, don't smoke, drink sensibly, minimise stress & mix socially.

SOCIAL

- people who play sport & are part of a club have a sense of belonging. They develop friendships with others in their team. Have the opportunity to make new friends & interact with other players, managers, coaches on & off pitch. Being with others make alleviate loneliness as they are part of a wider group & can mix socially. Particularly important OAPs.

EMOTIONAL (not mental!)

exercise releases endorphins. Produces 'serotonin'. Regulates mood, anxiety & happiness. Makes you feel good. Active people, more likely to have good self image. Think they look good.

Overweight/obese - less likely. More likely to have good self esteem. Push yourself to achieve a goal → feel good eg run a marathon.

Challenge physically & psychologically. Exercise can relieve stress after a hard day at work. Endorphins. Forget about the day, unwind.

Overweight → Poor Body Image → Low Self Esteem → Isolation

Anxiety → Depression → No Social Mixing

PHYSICAL

- improve all areas of fitness especially CVE, MS & ME. Can also improve social & emotional wellbeing → lead a healthy active lifestyle. Activity means...

- Less chance of injury through stronger muscles, ligaments & tendons.

- Good CVE will reduce risk of Coronary Heart Disease. Exercise prevents arteries from thickening.

+ improves MS & ME

weight bearing activity + weight training reduces risk of osteoporosis in later life. - improves bone density

healthy heart through good diet & activity - reduces risk of obesity & diabetes (type II) - extremely obesity / overweight 20% of 30% of - linked to better posture. Less issues in later life - load back. - muscle/skeletal damage

more likely - inactive

- associated decrease in blood pressure less strain on the heart

36

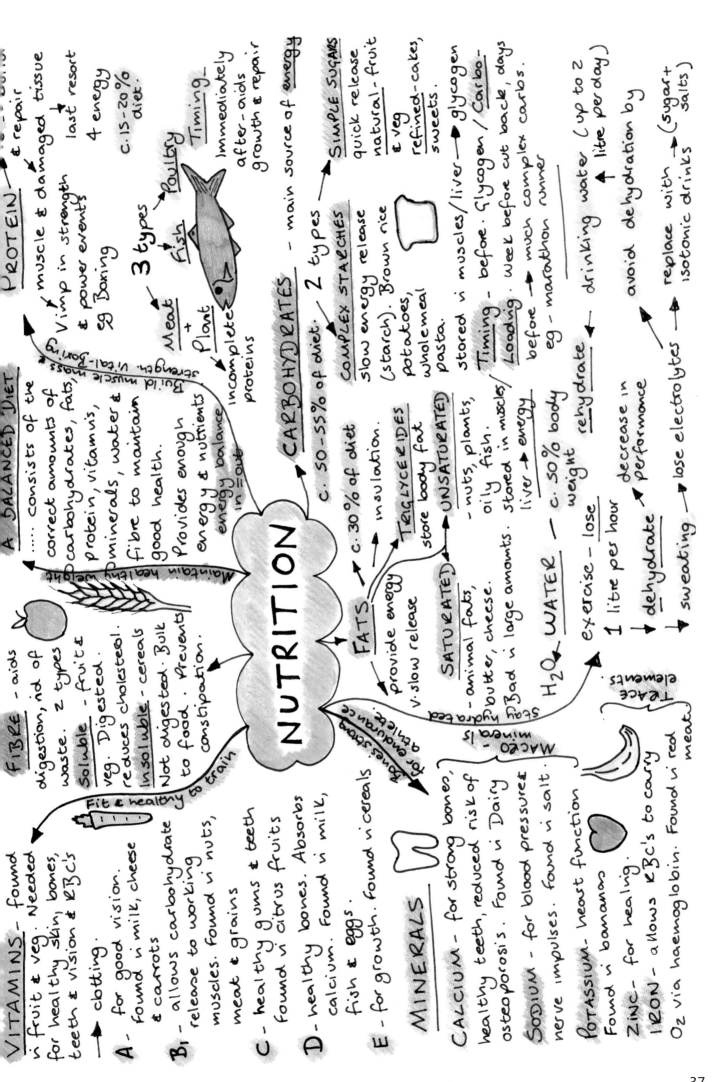

NUTRITION

A BALANCED DIET
..... consists of the correct amounts of carbohydrates, fats, protein, vitamins, minerals, water & fibre to maintain good health. Provides enough energy & nutrients. energy balance in = out

Maintain healthy weight
Build muscle, strength, vital mass. Eg - Boxing

PROTEIN - & repair
↑ muscle & damaged tissue
↑ imp in strength & power events eg Boxing
4 energy
last resort → 4 energy
c. 15-20% diet

Timing - Immediately after - aids growth & repair

3 types
→ Poultry
→ Fish
→ Meat + Plant → incomplete proteins

CARBOHYDRATES - main source of energy
c. 50-55% of diet
2 types

SIMPLE SUGARS
quick release
natural - fruit & veg
refined - cakes, sweets

COMPLEX STARCHES
slow energy release (starch). Brown rice potatoes, wholemeal pasta.
stored in muscles/liver → glycogen

Timing - before - Glycogen/Carbo-Loading. Week before cut back, days before → much complex carbs. eg - marathon runner

FATS
provide energy v. slow release

SATURATED
- animal fats, butter, cheese.
Bad in large amounts.

UNSATURATED
- nuts, plants, oily fish.
stored in muscles/liver → energy

store body fat
insulation.

TRIGLYCERIDES
c. 30% of diet

WATER - H₂O
c. 50% body weight
exercise - lose → rehydrate
1 litre per hour
dehydrate → decrease in performance
sweating → lose electrolytes
Stay hydrated → rehydrate
avoid dehydration by drinking water (up to 2 litre per day)
replace with isotonic drinks (sugar + salts)

MINERALS
Trace elements
MACRO minerals

CALCIUM - for strong bones, healthy teeth, reduced risk of osteoporosis. Found in Dairy
SODIUM - for blood pressure, nerve impulses. Found in salt.
POTASSIUM - heart function. Found in bananas
ZINC - for healing.
IRON - allows RBC's to carry O₂ via haemoglobin. Found in red meat

VITAMINS - found in fruit & veg. Needed for healthy skin, bones, teeth & vision & RBC's
A - for good vision. clotting. Found in milk, cheese & carrots
B - allows carbohydrate release to working muscles. Found in nuts, meat & grains
C - healthy gums & teeth. Found in citrus fruits
D - healthy bones. Absorbs calcium. Found in milk, fish & eggs.
E - for growth. Found in cereals

FIBRE - aids digestion, rid of waste. 2 types
Soluble - fruit & veg. Digested. reduces cholesterol.
Insoluble - cereals. Not digested. Bulk to food. Prevents constipation.

Fit & healthy to train
Remain strong & maintain performance as athlete

NOTES

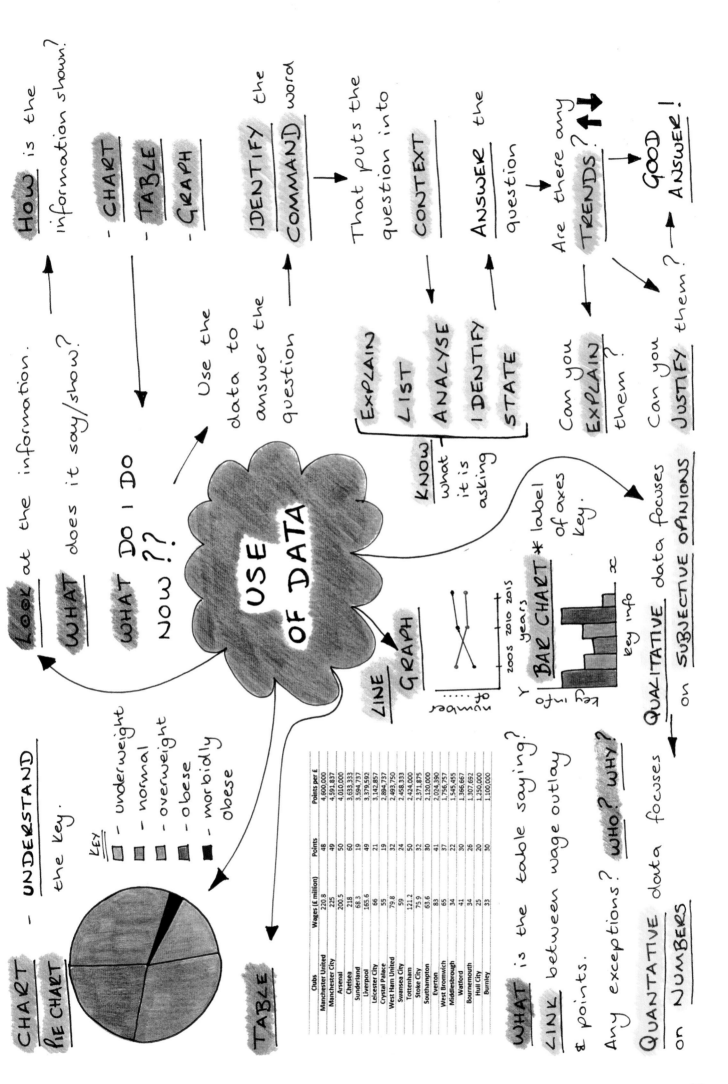

How is the information shown?
- CHART
- TABLE
- GRAPH

Look at the information.

WHAT does it say/show?

WHAT DO I DO NOW??

Use the data to answer the question

IDENTIFY the COMMAND word

That puts the question into CONTEXT

ANSWER the question

Are there any TRENDS?

GOOD ANSWER!

EXPLAIN
LIST
ANALYSE
IDENTIFY
STATE

KNOW what it is asking

Can you EXPLAIN them?

Can you JUSTIFY them?

USE OF DATA

CHART
PIE CHART

UNDERSTAND the key.

KEY
- underweight
- normal
- overweight
- obese
- morbidly obese

LINE GRAPH

number of ......to

2005 2010 2015
years

BAR CHART * label of axes key.

Y
key info

on QUALITATIVE data focuses on SUBJECTIVE OPINIONS

TABLE

WHAT is the table saying?

LINK between wage outlay & points.

Any exceptions? WHO? WHY?

QUANTITATIVE data focuses on NUMBERS

Clubs	Wages (£ million)	Points	Points per £
Manchester United	220.8	48	4,600,000
Manchester City	225	49	4,591,837
Arsenal	200.5	50	4,010,000
Chelsea	218	60	3,633,333
Sunderland	68.3	19	3,594,737
Liverpool	165.6	49	3,379,592
Leicester City	66	21	3,142,857
Crystal Palace	55	19	2,894,737
West Ham United	79.8	32	2,493,750
Swansea City	59	24	2,458,333
Tottenham	121.2	50	2,424,000
Stoke City	75.9	32	2,371,875
Southampton	63.6	30	2,120,000
Everton	83	41	2,024,390
West Bromwich	65	37	1,756,757
Middlesbrough	34	22	1,545,455
Watford	41	30	1,366,667
Bournemouth	34	26	1,307,692
Hull City	25	20	1,250,000
Burnley	33	30	1,100,000

39

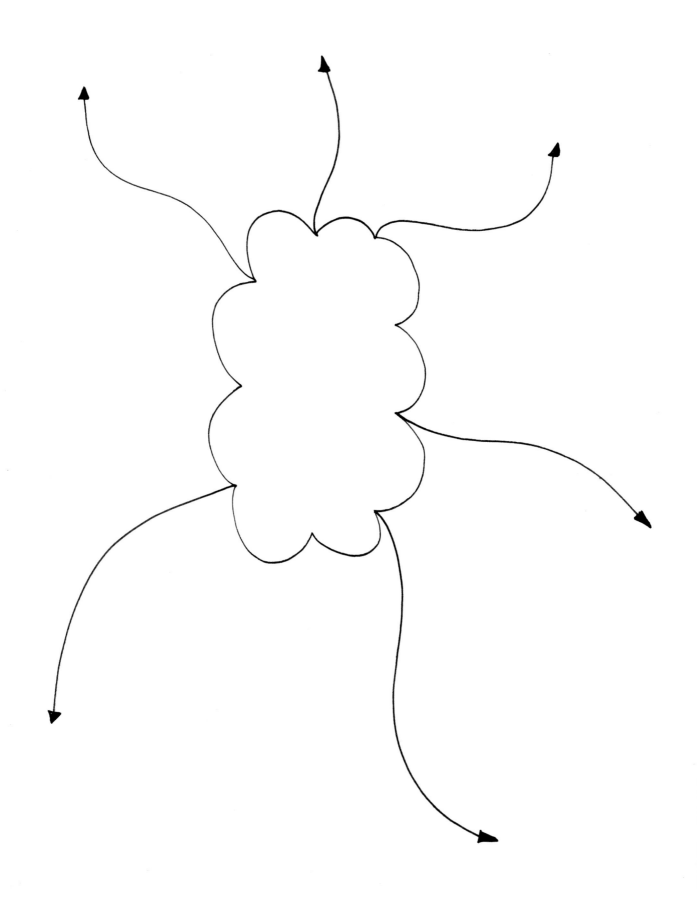

EXTENDED ANSWER QUESTIONS

① per paper, marked out of **6**. Content & answers may go across components.

AO2 = 4 marks
AO3 = 2 marks
= 6 marks total

When you look at the question, split it down into 3. Highlight the **KEY WORDS**

COMMAND word
TOPIC
CONTEXT

Linkage between the AOs is key!

COMMAND word tells you how to answer the Q.

Analyse
Discuss
Evaluate
Justify

the most commonly used command words for extended answer questions.

this works for all questions, not just extended.

TOPIC - this is the subject the answer is based on. eg- balanced diet.

CONTEXT - how the question relates to the topic. eg- 'balanced diet for an endurance athlete.'

These are the Assessment Objectives your answer must address.

AO1 - Demonstrate Knowledge & Understanding

AO2 - Apply Knowledge & Understanding.

AO3 - Analyse & evaluate the factors that underpin...

No marks, but help lead the answer into your AO2 section. Then link to AO3 to make your answer well constructed & persuasive. fluent - linkage.

NOTES